MW00884309

# ARE YOU A WIFE OR A KNIFE?

## Are you building him up or cutting him up?

### BY VEDIA R. JACKSON

Copyright © 2009 by Vedia R. Jackson

*Are You A Wife Or A Knife?*
by Vedia R. Jackson

Printed in the United States of America

ISBN 9781615794089

All rights reserved solely by the author. The author guarantees all contents are original and do not infringe upon the legal rights of any other person or work. No part of this book may be reproduced in any form without the permission of the author. The views expressed in this book are not necessarily those of the publisher.

Bible quotations are taken from the King James Version.
Book Cover Created by InLine Design orders@uneeditwhen.com

www.xulonpress.com

To
Jamari,

Be Blessed

Love Ya,

Pastor Kedia Joees

# Table of Contents

Breaking the Ice ........................................................7

Word on the Streets ...................................................8

Can We Talk? ...........................................................11

Well Done Please ......................................................13

Smooth Operator .......................................................15

Off With His Head! ....................................................17

Double Teaming ........................................................19

Stick 'Em Up! ..........................................................21

Mrs. Jekyll & Mrs. Hyde ..............................................23

Here Comes the Bride....................................................25

Will the Real Mrs._____Please Stand Up? ...........................28

Chopped Liver ..........................................................30

United We Stand, Divided We Fall .....................................32

Get A Handle On Yourself .............................................34

The Sword of the Spirit.....................................................36

Can We Talk Some More? .............................................38

Testimonies .....................................................................39

Conclusion ......................................................................41

The Man's Point of View: The Sharpener......................43

# Breaking The Ice

Are You a Wife or a Knife? I'm sure the question sounds pretty funny. It sounded funny to me the first time I heard it. This book is a result of a conference message that I've been teaching around the nation. I do not advocate divorce. I advocate change. This book is for those who want change. It proves that God has His own special way of dealing with each of us. If we'll let Him, He'll cleanse our hearts, change our lives, and use us to help others along the way. We must pass the wisdom in God's Word concerning marriage down to our daughters. With instruction and impartation, they will be able to enjoy the life that God provides. I guarantee that as you read this book and embrace the message, your life and the lives of those you share it with will be changed forever.

Pastor Vedia Jackson

# The Word on the Streets

People everywhere are discussing the rate of divorce within the body of Christ when it shouldn't even be named among us! God's Word tells us that He "hates divorce." As Christians, we should hate it too. You might say, "Pastor Vedia, I love God and I love my husband, but I can't stay in this marriage with a distant man who never does anything!" I'm sure you do love God, Sister! Just hold on tight and I'll share with you the secrets to a long healthy marriage – the way that God shared it with me. This message might not make you shout or holler, but if you take this information and use it, you'll see God's ability to work out every situation in your marriage and family relationships.

I'm going to break the ice by telling on myself. I grew up in a home where love and affection weren't commonly shown. After a stressful divorce from my father, my mother took her pain into a second marriage. Because of this, I learned marriage survival tactics instead of principles that would help me to overcome. I was taught to never allow a man to make a fool of me. I was told, "You should never let a man know everything about you." I also learned to keep a little money on the side in my own bank account that my husband couldn't touch. I was taught to protect myself by living a divorced life without the divorce papers!

As I got older, I lived by what I was taught. I got married at an early age and it didn't work out the way I planned. Years later, after getting saved, I promised myself and God that I would be the best Christian wife ever - if He would just send me a good Christian man. When my "good Christian man" came into the picture, I knew things had to be different this time around. I wanted my new marriage to be the type of marriage that God wanted for me. I wanted my new husband to feel appreciated. I just didn't know how to get what I was hoping for.

The first few years with my new husband were sometimes very rough – especially when my husband tried to correct me! I grew up in poverty. And in public housing, you don't just get away with saying something that we didn't like. We'd cut you up with words in a minute! They were our defense. You might just get cut with something other than words! I was taught to be a fighter – to guard my soft spots and be tough with anybody who thought they were big and bad enough to step to me. I had the same defensive attitude with my husband. I didn't want to have that attitude toward him, but I was never taught Proverbs 14:1 which says: *"Every wise woman buildeth her house: but the foolish plucketh it down with her hands."*

When my husband would say something I didn't like, I would tear him down with my words. If he confronted me about anything, I took it personally. I would feel rejected – even when he was right. Now don't get me wrong, I wouldn't cuss him out – I was a Christian woman! But I would be sure to "pluck" him down with the words of my mouth so he would back off. I would say things like, "Your not my Father! I was grown when you met me!" Or I'd say, "I don't know, maybe you married the wrong woman. Maybe I should have just stayed single!" He would just stand there staring at me with his eyes filled with hurt. I was giving my mouth over to Satan, unaware that I was also giving my marriage over to him. After too many of my verbal attacks, my husband would give up and walk away. This went on for a while until I watched my husband become totally detached from me.

I'd pray, "Lord, You know I'm trying to be the best wife I can be! You know all the baggage my husband brought into this marriage. I'm doing everything I know to do, Lord, but when he says he's going to do something, he doesn't do it. He never keeps his word.

I've been praying for him for a long time now, Lord. You gotta do something!"

One day, the Lord said to me, "Vedia, this is not a prayer for your husband. This is you trying to convince Me that you're not the problem." I answered, "Look what I'm doing, Jesus. I'm praying to You!" "No," He said. "Nothing will change like this. You have to be honest with Me." He asked me, "Vedia Jackson, are you a wife or a knife?"

I was like, "Wait a minute. Is that You, God?" (You know how we like to get spiritual when it seems like we're about to get corrected by the Holy Spirit.) I said, "If that's You, Lord, I need You to back it up with Scripture." Of course He did! He showed me Proverbs 30:14: *"There is a generation, whose teeth are as swords, and their jaw teeth as knives, to devour the poor from off the earth, and the needy from among men."*

He also took me to Proverbs 12:18: *"There is that speaketh like the piercing of a sword: but the tongue of the wise is health."*

I would be laying hands on my husband, praying over him and rebuking the devil when he caught the flu. But I was contradicting myself by speaking evil over him when he made me mad. God corrected me. He said, "Your husband is a man of God. Don't talk to My man like that." He showed me that if I continued, I would ultimately run my husband away. I found out that it was time to make some changes. I had to allow God to correct some things within me. It was time to renew my mind.

# Can We Talk?

There are two types of communication: vocal and non-vocal. In vocal communication, we use our words and tone of voice. For example, our words may be harsh and communicated with a harsh tone. Or they may be peaceful with a peaceful tone. In nonverbal communication, we use our facial expressions and body language to get our points across: We may roll our eyes and flip our hands. Or smile and keep our arms and hands neutral. Both types of communication are a result of what we have in our hearts. In Matthew 12:34, Jesus tells us that we speak *"out of the abundance of our hearts."* A good wife, *"out of the abundance of good in her heart will speak good things"* to her husband. But an evil wife, *"out of the abundance of evil things in her heart will speak evil things"* to her husband. I have counseled so many women who just can't figure out why their husbands won't share their feelings. I have found that a woman's words, her actions, her tone of voice, and how she comes across all play a vital role in her interaction with her husband. If a wife communicates improperly with her husband, he may become detached like my husband did. God answered my prayers by giving me a good Christian man for a husband. But my heart was filled with issues. I didn't love or accept myself, so it was hard for me to love and accept my husband. I had to make myself available to God so that He could deal with my issues!

"Okay, okay, Lord," I prayed. "It's me! I'm the one with the low self-esteem and the character flaws! I'm the one with all the issues and the extra baggage!"

When I was honest and open with God, He began to heal me. After He healed my heart issues, He gave me the responsibility to counsel and minister to others. When I started counseling other women, sharing with them the big "Are You a Wife or a Knife?" question, God showed me the different types of knives a wife can be to her husband. If you find that you've been more of a knife than a wife as you read, don't get condemned! Just know that you're in the right place for God to deal with your heart. Repent and ask Him to help you change your approach.

# WELL DONE PLEASE
## The Steak Knife Wife

The first knife is the type of knife I used to be. It's the Steak Knife. I wanted my husband to be just like my steak: well done! I wanted him spiritually mature, mature in his faith walk. I wanted him to be perfect! Anytime he showed imperfections, I took out my steak knife mentality, cut his manhood into bite size pieces, then chewed him up and spat him out.

Like many married women today, I used to forget how to appreciate the little things that my husband did for me. Wife: "Honey, take out the garbage!"

Husband: "I did take the garbage out."

Wife: "You left this box! You can't do anything right!"

When we don't appreciate the small things, we rob our husbands of the respect they need to get the job done completely. Attacking them for mistakes will cut into, and tear away the substance of our marriage relationships the way steak knives cut into meat.

Ladies, our husbands are much more than meat! The Holy Spirit showed me Matthew 25:21. It says:

*"His lord said unto him, well done, thou good and faithful servant: thou hast been faithful over a few things, I will make thee ruler over many things: enter thou into the joy of thy lord."*

Jesus is Lord of my husband's life. He's the one who will one day say to my husband, "Well done, my faithful servant." Not me! I'm not to be my husband's judge or critic. Instead, I have to be the one who builds him up with wise words. If I am faithful to build him up with wise words, God will entrust me with greater things.

**The cure for a Steak Knife Wife:**
1. Appreciate him and thank him for the little things.
2. Avoid the temptation of being his worst critic.

# SMOOTH OPERATOR
## The Butter Knife Wife

*"For the lips of a strange woman drop as a honeycomb, and her mouth is smoother than oil..."* Proverbs 5:3

The Butter Knife Wife is smoooooth! She's good at working her husband over to get exactly what she wants. At certain times of the month, she has a headache-until she spots a designer purse in the mall! That's when she turns on the charm. She cooks his favorite meal, compliments him, and butters him up. She'll say, "Baby you're so fine. Are you losing weight?" (When she knows he's bigger than ever!) The Butter Knife Wife is a master planner and manipulator. She knows her husband's pay schedule well. When the paycheck is on the way, she's eager to work it! She's ready to give him whatever he wants so that she can benefit. Her poor husband thinks that he is finally getting an answer to his prayers, since his Butter Knife Wife hasn't touched him in weeks. But once her desires are fulfilled and she gets the designer purse, she goes right back to withholding herself from him physically and emotionally.

We cannot expect God to get involved when we're being manipulative like this. It may not be a dress or a purse. It may be a house. It may be a car. No matter what it is that we want, the way we go about getting it has to be free of manipulation. Our actions toward our husbands have to be motivated by love – not material desires. Besides, Psalm 37:4 says that we are to *"delight in the Lord"* and

He will provide us with the *"desires of our hearts."* God may use our husbands, but we are to look to Him to receive the things we ask of Him.

**The cure for a Butter Knife Wife:**
1. Allow love to be the motivation for every action.
2. Look to God to supply your desires and needs.

# OFF WITH HIS HEAD!

## The Butcher Knife Wife

Next, we have the Butcher Knife Wife. The Butcher Knife Wife is ruthless! She's brutal! She'll chop her husband up with her words then say, "I'm just speaking the truth." In reality, she's brutally and hurtfully honest. When her husband comes home from sweating at work for the family, she'll say things like, "You stink!" Or "Look how you dress. You're so old fashioned!" Or "You're always broke!"

The worst thing about the Butcher Knife Wife is that she'll talk to her husband this way in private and in public! Her husband is almost afraid to talk with her in front of others at times because she easily forgets that he has feelings and he doesn't want to be embarrassed in front of family and friends. She chops and guts out his emotions in front of all, not realizing that she's also cutting away his feelings for her. After constantly butchering her husband and embarrassing him, a Butcher Knife Wife will eventually cause her husband to shut down. Once he shuts down, he may even become cold towards her. If your husband is cold towards you, could it be that you've chopped him up? Colossians 4:6 says: *"Let your speech be always with grace, seasoned with salt, that ye may know how ye ought to answer every man."*

As women of God, our speech must be full of God's grace to comfort and bring out the best in our husbands. Proverbs 25:11 says: *"A word fitly spoken is like apples of gold in pictures of silver."*

If we desire to please God, we have to be honest and truthful with our spouses, but the time and place that we choose to be honest - as well as the tone of voice we use - must be carefully chosen. Remember ladies, our husbands desire to have our respect and the respect of the people around them. It may be hard to bite your tongue at times, but for the sake of your marriage, hold onto the truth and allow God to show you how to present it properly.

**The cure for a Butcher Knife Wife:**
1. Give your husband some good old-fashioned R-E-S-P-E-C-T!
2. Avoid "telling him off" or exposing him in public.
3. Ask God to help you present the truth with humility.

# DOUBLE TEAMING

## The Paring Knife Wife

*"Wherefore they are no more twain, but one flesh. What therefore God hath joined together, let not man put asunder."*
- Matthew 19:6

The paring knife has a short blade, which is a representation of the Paring Knife Wife's short temper. She uses everything she has to get under her husband's skin and peel it away. She brings others in to fill his place in her life, cutting him out and refusing to allow him to cover and protect her. She shares secrets with her friends, her mother – even her Pastor, but when it comes to her husband, she remains separate. She will even go as far as pairing up with her children against her husband. She will go against her husband's advice, structure and principles just to show others that she's in control. For example, her husband may not approve of their daughter wearing a certain shirt, skirt or tight jeans, but instead of trusting her husband's judgment, she'll ask her daughter how she feels with the outfit on. If the daughter says she feels fine, the Paring Knife Wife will side with her daughter. At that point, the Paring Knife Wife has destroyed the authority that her husband has established in their home. This is a big mistake for the Paring Knife Wife. When overwhelming issues arise in the home she'll need her husband to use his authority to make things better. But she has forgotten that she has undermined his standards and stripped him of his ability to get the job done. She has unknowingly trained her children to second-guess his decisions. The problems in their home go unsolved because she has literally robbed her husband of their children's respect. You can always tell a Paring Knife Wife's husband by the way he is detached. He'll come in and eat dinner with the family – but he won't say a word. He'll go into a room alone and stay for hours because he doesn't feel like he's a part of her life. I met a young lady who could never understand her husband's detachment. She was devastated by it. She allowed her short temper to rule her conversations with her husband for years. She constantly attacked him verbally until he divorced her. She never knew the root of her problems with her husband until she realized that she was a Paring Knife Wife. By then, it was too late.

If we slice our husbands out of our lives and give their position to others, we'll ultimately hurt ourselves. In Genesis 2:23, Adam called his wife, *"bone of my bone, and flesh of my flesh."* Just imagine a tooth being abstracted without any Novocain, the terrible pain of replacement surgery without anesthesia! It would be traumatic! This is the type of emotional trauma that we experience when we slice our husbands out of our lives and replace them with others. Our husbands are vital pieces of our lives – we have to be careful not to let others into to the places that only our husbands should occupy.

**The cure for a Paring Knife Wife:**
1. Avoid filling your husband's place in your life with another (even your children).
2. Control your short temper.
3. Ask God to help you become one with your husband again.
4. If there is a discrepancy, talk to him in private

# STICK 'EM UP!

## The Pocket Knife Wife

*"There is treasure to be desired, and oil in the dwelling of the wise; but a foolish man spendeth it up."*- Proverbs 21:20

The Pocket Knife Wife is the woman who stays in her husband's pockets. She's the wife that will take the money her husband gives her for the light bill and spend it on a new outfit. Even though she hides the new clothes in the trunk or in the back of her closet, the truth always comes out because her family has to eat by candle light at the end of the month. This is the lady who never gets enough. She'll spot something in a furniture store or at the mall and that's it – she's gotta have it! The next thing you know her husband is trying to make a business call on his cell phone and the phone isn't working and they're about to be thrown out of their home because she had to get a new couch and some designer sneakers for the baby. Over a period of time, her family experiences financial ruin because of her lack of self-control.

Regardless of her husband's financial vision, the Pocket Knife Wife craves something new every week. Her family never gets to a solid financial destination because she can't wait to get her hands on the latest fashion power.

Proverbs 21:20 calls the Pocket Knife Wife's actions *"foolish."* Though her husband may be a wise man, the Pocket Wife Knife's family is always a day late and a dollar short. Her husband cannot trust her because of her irrational spending and dishonesty. It could be that she has a problem with covetousness. She may have insecurities that she believes materialism can cure. It may be a bad case of "comparsonitis". No matter what her issue may be, Luke 12:15 says:

*"And He said to them, "Take heed and beware of covetousness, for a man's life consisteth not in the abundance of the things which he possesseth".*

**The cure for a Pocket Knife Wife:**
1. Appreciate the little things and be a good steward over them.
2. Check with your husband before you spend (agreement is important).
3. Ask God to free your heart from materialism.

# MRS. JEKYLL & MRS. HYDE
## The Switch Blade Wife

*"For he that wavereth is like a wave of the sea driven with the wind and tossed. For let not that man think that he shall receive any thing of the Lord. A double minded man is unstable in all his ways."*
                                                        - James 1:6-8

The Switch Blade Wife is double-minded. This makes her emotionally dangerous! She's moody – even when it's not "that time of the month." Her mood changes are a normal part of her personality. The Switch Blade Wife's husband has no idea of how to deal with her from one day to the next because she has no stability. She loves her husband today; but he better look out because her mood might shift tomorrow. If something goes wrong at work, she'll come home and take her frustration out on her family. Her poor husband always ends up confused because he's unsure of how to handle her unstable mindset. "She loves me, she loves me not," is his daily song. James 1:8 calls this type of wife *"double-minded and unstable in all her ways."* It goes on to explain that this type of woman can't expect to receive anything from God because of her instability. In Mark 14:36, Jesus had to deal with the temptation to be double-minded through prayer: *"And he said, Abba, Father, all things are possible unto thee; take away this cup from me: nevertheless not what I will, but what thou wilt."*

Jesus' own will wasn't to go to the cross! But He submitted His will to the Father's will. The Switch Blade Wife must get in God's Word on a daily basis so that her mind can be transformed, or renewed according to Romans 12:2. When we spend time renewing our minds in God's Word and worshipping Him, we purify our hearts so that our double will becomes one with God's will.

**The cure for a Switch Blade Wife:**
1. Cast your cares on the Lord - especially after work.
2. Submit your emotions to God daily.
3. Allow your will to become one with God's will.

**"Here comes the bride, here comes the bride... Have you ever-seen how beautifully the cake knife is decorated?"**

# The Cake Knife Wife

*"Favor is deceitful, and beauty is vain but a woman that fears the Lord, she shall be praised."*
- Proverbs 31:30

Here comes the bride, here comes the bride... Have you ever seen how beautifully the cake knife is decorated? The only thing the Cake Knife Wife brings to the table is her beauty. She only intends for her husband to decorate her with the finest. It is all about status with this woman. She knows she has to find the right man who is able to buy her the material things she desires or feels she needs. Once she finds a man who is up for the job, she quickly strikes him with her beauty (and every other physical feature that can lure a man) because she knows she is only working with a limited amount of time. It is very important not to underestimate the Cake Knife Wife because she has done her men-and-what-they-like homework. The Cake Knife Wife's husband loves to show her off at barbeques, company parties and everywhere his friends gather together because they consider him to be "The Man." His wife knows and understands the game very well and she continues to play because she is there to be in the spotlight with all eyes on her. The Cake Knife Wife is just Arm and Eye Candy. Her husband's got the money and she's got the beauty.

Working is not an option for this wife. She feels that going to part-time work or going to a 9 to 5 is beneath her. She does not want to clean the house or wash dishes. She even gives the nanny her primary responsibilities with her children because she's too busy "keeping up with the Joneses" and getting her beauty sleep. Making love with her husband is a chore instead of a priority - she can take it or leave it. She is only around to look pretty and to be ready for special occasions. The Cake Knife Wife spends her time searching through fashion magazines, keeping up with the latest fashions and getting her hair, nails and pedicures done.

This wife enjoys dressing provocatively to go out on the town and have a good time with her husband. Things are great when he's giving her what she wants. But he knows their relationship will come to an end if he shows that he can't keep up with her high maintenance profile or if he no longer wants to contribute to her excessive need for material things. What the Cake Knife Wife doesn't understand is that there comes a time when a man will require her to do more than just look pretty. He will need her support on tough decisions concerning his job or other critical life-changing events. He may also need her financial support. Once her husband finds out that his Cake Knife Wife isn't capable of giving him the support he needs, the marriage experiences an extreme storm. He realizes that his Cake Knife Wife cannot handle the storm and that he has chosen the wrong type of woman.

Unfortunately, a man who dates a woman like this will lose all possibilities of marriage if he doesn't keep the perks coming. If he has grown to love her, it will be difficult for him to shake her because he's stuck on her beauty and the sexual fulfillment that she gave to him. If he's strong enough, he may just walk out on her. If the Cake Knife Wife does not get true deliverance - which only comes from

God – she will never find true happiness. She will seek men for approval and material things to fill her voids for the rest of her life.

**The cure for a Cake Knife Wife:**
1. Seek God for approval instead of man.
2. Know that you are more than just a pretty face. (Believe in yourself!)
3. Become more than just your husband's trophy.
4. Become a blessing to your husband – not a burden.

# WILL THE REAL MRS. PLEASE STAND UP?

## The Plastic Knife Wife

*"Behold, thou desirest truth in the inward parts: and in the hidden part thou shalt make me to know wisdom."* -Psalm 51:6

The Plastic Knife Wife is the phony wife. When I say, "phony," I'm not talking about hair extensions, false eyelashes or acrylic nails. (You know we have to get our nails done!) When I say she's phony, I mean she refuses to be herself. Instead of being the woman who God created her to be, she takes in what other people expect from her and makes them her own expectations. When it comes to her husband, the Plastic Knife Wife won't stand up to him. Instead of being honest and saying, "It hurts me when you talk to me like that," she'll hold it in and pretend everything is okay. In Psalm 51:6 we learn that God desires truth even in the *"inward parts"*; therefore, we cannot hide the truth and pretend that everything is okay.

Another type of Plastic Knife Wife is the lady who doesn't mind living in false prosperity. She likes to make others believe that her marriage is great and that her money is right. She'll go into work and tell all of her girlfriends that she just came back from a spring break trip with her family when she knows she didn't go anywhere! This phony lady likes to keep her outer image in top shape. She'll go as far as pressuring her husband to bring in more money just so she can keep the show going. What's funny about the Plastic Knife Wife is that with all the pressure she puts on her husband, she can't hold up under the slightest bit of pressure. She can't take the heat because she's plastic – just like the plastic knife. In the heat of her trials, she'll give up and call it quits. She and her husband never deal with root issues because the Plastic Knife Wife can't handle it. She'll live a life of facades rather than face reality head on.

You may know a Plastic Knife Wife. You may be one yourself. Though they are very entertaining, the plastic Knife Wife's attributes are not from God. Any attributes that are not from God are strange to Him – they just don't fit in His plans. God calls us to be virtuous women – full of His power. He requires us to be truthful. He doesn't want us to look like the truth and act like the truth but never bear fruit. God wants us to be fruitful in our hearts as well as in our actions. When we bear fruits of righteousness, we can help others to cultivate the same fruit in their own lives.

## *The cure for a Plastic Knife Wife:*
1. Stop pretending.
2. Be real (with God, your family, and your friends).
3. Don't run away from trouble; learn how to overcome them. (Learn to trouble your trouble!)

# CHOPPED LIVER

## The Meat Cleaver Knife Wife

*"He that is soon angry dealeth foolishly: and a man of wicked devices is hated."*- Proverbs 14:17

We've been discussing how our words and actions can cut into our relationships like knives. But one day, while teaching this message at a women's conference, the Lord told me to add the Meat Cleaver Wife. "A Meat Cleaver Wife?" I asked. "Lord, You sure?" He showed me that there are some women that have spirits filled with violence. These women actually use physical knives to cut their husbands' flesh. The Meat Cleaver Wife has layers of hurt from physical abuse - a violent background that causes her to threaten her husband's life.

One woman shared with me that she grew up fighting with knives in a gang. She was trained to defend herself when she felt threatened. Sometime before she was married, she was the victim in an abusive relationship, which kept her on edge. Once she was married, her defensive mindset hadn't changed. Anytime her husband would come at her in a way she felt was offensive, she'd become angry and threaten him with knives. She even cut him a few times. As she shared her story with me, she cried and repented for allowing her violent past to get the best of her.

There are thousands of other women who have dealt with this. There are women in prison who have been convicted for acts of violence against their husbands. Some have even committed murder. Some have turned the violence toward themselves and used suicide as a way out.

Ladies, we should never allow ourselves to be pushed so far. We don't have to use ungodly ways to get our points across to our husbands. We don't have to use weapons or cut them down with what we say. In 2 Corinthians 10: 4, Paul says that the *"weapons of our warfare are not carnal."* There is no need to use what the world uses! There is no test or trial that is too hard for God to fix. He can come into any circumstance
and turn it around for our benefit. It only takes surrendering to Him. When we surrender to God, He gives us the same ability to turn circumstances around for others.

## The cure for a Meat Cleaver Wife:
1. Never threaten your husband's physical or emotional safety.
2. Ask others for help.
3. Learn ways to manage your anger.

# UNITED WE STAND, DIVIDED WE FALL...

## The Scissor Wife

*"And Jesus knew their thoughts, and said unto them, every kingdom divided against itself is brought to desolation; and every city or house divided against itself shall not stand..."* -Matthew 12:25

The Scissor Wife is the woman who always snips her husband's plans in two. Her husband works hard to come up with plans for the household budget or a new business; but the Scissor Wife takes one look at his plans and cuts them right up. Sometimes she won't even give her husband her respect by listening to the entire plan before she starts snipping.

A Scissor Wife only trusts her own plans. She refuses to go with what her husband thinks is best because she believes that her ideas are better. Her favorite input begins with, "That's okay, but..." Once her husband helps her obtain her degree or another goal that she has planned out, she cuts herself off from him. Their accomplishments and the things they've acquired together no longer belong to both of them. They become all hers.

Scissors are good for cutting out patterns. They do come in handy, but as a woman of God, we are to follow our husband's pattern without cutting into them. You may ask, "Pastor Vedia, what if he makes a mistake?" You must understand that mistakes are not failures. Men confirm their identity in what they do. When God formed Adam, he woke up in the Garden of Eden. The Lord took the man and put him in the Garden of Eden to work it and take care of it. Men look for something to accomplish. They just need some one to believe in them. What they miss in the natural, we as wives can help them catch in the Spirit. One thing I know for sure is that men want to hear, "I believe in you." These words are like medicine to them.

When they make mistakes, we should not penalize their mistakes forever! We make mistakes too! Our husbands need mercy for mistakes just as we do. When mistakes are made, we must exercise patience and trust. We should remember that the Word of God is able to correct all that is wrong.

## *The cure for a Scissor Wife:*
1. Listen to your husband's plans.
2. Trust that God will take care of any mistakes that are made.

# GET A HANDLE ON YOURSELF!
## The Dusty Rusty Knife Wife

*A virtuous woman is a crown to her husband: but she that maketh ashamed is as rottenness in his bone.* - Proverbs 12:4

The Dusty Rusty Wife has forgotten about her appearance! Before she was married, she was the sharpest lady in town. She wore the latest fashions. She kept her hair and nails done and she always had the latest perfume. When she got married, she got comfortable and she let herself go.

The Dusty Rusty Wife's husband is looking for the woman he married! He wonders what is happening to that fire they used to have. He wants to enjoy their time together but he is confused about why things aren't the same. The Dusty Rusty Knife Wife feels the tension and constantly prays asking God to save her marriage and rekindle the fire, but her daily appearance is unkempt and her bedtime clothes are undesirable! Instead of attraction, her appearance shows concern. There could be some depression. She may need some inner healing of some kind or maybe she needs some shopping money.

According to Proverbs, a wife is the "crown" of her husband. A man's crown should have some type of "bling"! We make our husbands proud when we look good for them. On top of that, we feel good about ourselves. Feeling good about who we are, makes us free to glorify God and to give love to our husbands. Looking good on the outside requires an inward makeover. 1 Peter 3:1-4 says:

*"Likewise, ye wives, be in subjection to your own husbands; that, if any obey not the word, they also may without the word be won by the conversation of the wives; while they behold your chaste conversation coupled with fear. Whose adorning let it not be that outward adorning of plaiting the hair, and of wearing of gold, or of putting on of apparel. But let it be the hidden man of the heart, in that which is not corruptible, even the ornament of a meek and quiet spirit, which is in the sight of God of great price."*

In this Scripture, we as wives are admonished to win our husbands over with our manner of living. It is the meekness of our hearts that will win our husbands over not our hardness of heart. When we're confident on the inside, it shows on the outside. We must not let ourselves go. We've got to keep ourselves meek on the inside and give our husbands something they can enjoy looking at on the outside.

## *The cure for a Dusty Rusty Knife Wife:*
1. Check your self-image.
2. Keep yourself looking good. (It'll help rekindle the flame.)

# THE SWORD OF THE SPIRIT
## The Spirit-Filled Wife

*"And take the helmet of salvation and the Sword of the Spirit which is the Word of God.*

- Ephesians 6:17

Ladies, this is the knife that we should never put away or allow to become dull. The Sword of the Spirit, the Word of God, will fight the devil's plans for our marriages. It will cut our enemies out of our finances, out of our families, out of our homes and out of our thoughts. We've been called "sharp dressers" when our shoes match our purses and when our hairstyles are just right. When we're dressed like that we wouldn't dare go out in public unless our nails are done too! Let's take on the same attitude regarding the Word of God! Let's get "fill-ins" every morning by filling ourselves with God's Word! Let's not leave the house dressed sharply on the outside without sharpening ourselves spiritually.

Hebrews 4:12 says: *" For the Word is living and powerful and sharper than any two-edge sword, piercing even to the division of soul and Spirit and joints and marrow and is a discerner of the thoughts and intents of the heart..."*

The Sword of the Spirit is a knife that God and most husbands would like for a wife to carry. She can use it no matter where she goes. Remember ladies: In the face of any obstacles, choose to use the Sword of the Spirit. It is the only knife that the devil hates to see you use! Though we are taught by society to become cold and militant when faced with tough situations, God sees a quiet spirit as strength. Isaiah 35:15 says: *"For thus says the Lord GOD, the Holy One of Israel: 'In returning and rest you shall be saved; in quietness and confidence shall be your strength..."* A meek and quiet spirit is a sign that we trust God. When we use the Sword of the Spirit by speaking His Word, it's a sign that we trust Him to take care of our needs. This allows God to supply us with good things and win our husbands hearts over. In this way, we will be victorious in every situation. God will lead us into triumph every time. Proverbs 14:1 says: "Every wise woman buildeth her house, but the foolish plucketh it down with her hands."

Men are usually expected to be the builders. But here in Proverbs 14, God calls women the *homebuilders.* We are responsible to build the atmosphere of our homes and to build up those who are in our homes. God is looking for some good women to build up – not cut up!

# Can We Talk Some More?

Marriage is the death of two wills and the covenant of one. Once we have allowed God to deal with our issues, our marriages will become fruitful. That's when two people can actually see eye to eye and flow as one.

A special type of communication results when two people are in harmony with one another. It's called, TACIT/TACIT. It is when a wife can give her husband a specific look and he knows exactly what she means without one word spoken. It's when a husband gives his wife one glance in a crowded room and she knows that he's ready to go.

TACIT/ TACIT is the type of harmony that comes when a wife studies her husband's likes and dislikes so closely that she knows when he's pleased and when he's not, just from his body language. This type of woman listens to her husband's voice when he's speaking and hears it even when he isn't saying a word.

TACIT/TACIT communication is reached by the willingness of both spouses. TACIT/TACIT isn't one sided and it's not rocket science! It takes time, effort, and the help of the Holy Spirit. All God asks for is willing vessels.

In Genesis 2:23, Adam calls Eve *"Bone of his bones and flesh of his flesh."* He continued to say that for this reason a man would leave his mother and father and cleave or cling to his wife. God expects us to cleave to our husbands as well. We cleave until we are meshed with them as one.

# Testimonies

**MARQUITE JOHNSON**, Chicago, IL

*The knife I most identified with was a Paring Knife. I was very short-tempered with my husband and I had an extremely flipped mouth. I asked GOD for a man like him, but when I got him I didn't understand that my words were cutting up my marriage. I attended classes where Pastor Vedia was our teacher. At first, I thought that none of the knives described me. But when Pastor Vedia began talking about the Paring Knife, I almost fell out of my seat! I felt like I was being exposed! Following Pastor Vedia's class instructions, I went home to repent. I told my husband about what I discovered in class that morning. We talked about it all night. It was shocking when my husband told me howhe really felt about the way I spoke to him. I apologized and promised to change. The teaching I receivedthat day has truly changed my life and the lives of the people around me. I never want to be seen as a utensil used against my husband. I want to be seen as a woman of God.*

**CHRISTINE MICKELS**

*Learning about the different knives helped me to see myself. I found out that I was a Paring Knife too. I would always pair up with my adult daughters and talk about their father. I had a way of showing my disapproval of my husband's actions by cutting my eyes at him. I can't say that I am completely changed, but now I understand that if I want my marriage to survive, I can't keep harming my husband with my mouth. The Wife or Knife message is helping me to change the way I treat my husband.*

**PAMELA PEETE**, Coral Springs, FL
*I used to feel so misunderstood by others. It kept me frustrated and afraid to be open and honest with my husband about how I really felt. I was always concerned about how he would receive what I had to say. During the Wife or Knife Session, I experienced another level of emotional healing. I learned that I shouldn't hold things in my heart just because I am afraid of my husband's response. I found that how I communicate with my husband is just as important as what I say. The words of wisdom that were shared helped me understand that I must promote, build and edify my husband through my words and trust that God is being glorified by what I say to him.*

**Lauren**, FL
*When I heard the Wife or Knife message, I was on the verge of signing divorce papers (after the service). I never thought that my mouth had destroyed my marriage, but after hearing about the different knives, I knew I was several of them. I met with my husband after the service to sign the papers and immediately began to cry. I apologized for all of the negative things I said over the years. He held me and forgave me. It was obvious that we still loved each other. I asked him if we could give it try again and he said yes! We are now in ministry together. Thanks Pastor Vedia!*

**ANN ELLIOT**, Ft. Lauderdale, FL
*During the first eight and a half years of my marriage, I never let my husband be himself. I realized it when I started to feel like I didn't even know who he was. I would hit him, and down his manhood whenever he didn't meet my expectations. I would belittle his plans and remind him of his failures. After a while, he wouldn't say anything when he came home from work and he wouldn't give me any affection. In the Wife or Knife Session, I learned that my husband had shut down because of my words and my actions. I felt terrible and I repented. My husband is talking to me more and sharing his goals with me. I am so grateful to God.*

# CONCLUSION

## A Note from Pastor Vedia

I can't tell you how thrilled my heart is, knowing that I no longer have to use my mouth as a defense against my husband. Jesus is my defense now. He's your defense too. I am ecstatic at the thought of being able to pass these Godly attributes down to all of my daughters. The whole purpose of this book is to help us to become transparent so that others can experience change and to stop the emotional bleeding and pain that are results of what we say with our mouths. Our purpose as wives is to love God and our mates. We are to reflect Jesus' character and likeness in all that we do!

Proverbs 31:10 says: *" Who can find a virtuous woman? For her price is far above rubies."* God wants us to be women of noble character. This will allow the healing to begin. You cannot erase the past; but you can affect your future in a positive way by being a Wife instead of a Knife. When you feel like cutting up, remember to cut into the devil's plans not your husband. This is what the Sword of the Spirit is for! If your husband has experienced too many wounds from the words you've spoken, apologize, love him unconditionally begin to affirm him as much as possible and speak kindness to his soul.

*Proverbs 31:26 She openeth her mouth with wisdom; and In her tongue Is the law of kindness.*

Now give him time to heal. Only God can make him whole again.

I'd like to thank God for giving me the revelation of this teaching and His Word. I would also like to thank my husband Pastor Samuel Jackson Jr, Pastor LaShaon Brooks, each of my daughters, son-in-law Kenneth Williams and all of my family and friends.

# A Man's Point of View:
# The Sharpener

## Comments
## by Senior Pastor Samuel Jackson Jr.

Today, my wife Vedia is a very sharp, lively, witty and a humorous individual. She can have you laughing and feeling good in her company. However, there was another side to her. During the early and middle stages of our sixteen-year marriage, I could never put my finger on why certain things caused Vedia to react so negatively. I thought I was okay. Like most men, I placed little value on good communication and gave high regard to work and other things. Vedia would complain over and over about my lack of communication skills. I had a hard time accepting her view. I was self-centered and full of pride. My lack of sensitivity and unwillingness to take her seriously brought the worst out of her. Vedia would ask me, "Will you please let me know when you're leaving the house?" I found that hard to do, so I wouldn't tell her. I would also spend money without talking to her about it. I did this over and over and it made her very angry. I discovered a side of my wife that I could not defend myself from. It would make a grown man's feelings hurt to the point of tears. No matter how I tried to come back at her, she was sharper and quicker when cutting me up! Did I deserve it? Maybe or maybe not; however, her response didn't have to be such an over reaction. She became a Butcher Knife Wife to protect herself and I was using my words against her as well. We were using our words to hurt each other badly.

As we grew, we learned more about each other. I began to read books and listen to audio material on marriage. I finally realized that my communication skills really were terrible. My unwillingness to tell her where I was going, when I was leaving or how much I was going to spend were a sign of bad communication and poor integrity. As a Christian man, I had to accept that I was underdeveloped and immature in these areas of my life. I was dysfunctional in my communication.

Most men are not taught that good communication is a must for a woman's heart. It is unfortunate because wives will continue to be "knives" until men are aware of the need for good communication. Communication is as pleasing to a woman as physical satisfaction is to a man. Men get very angry when there isn't enough physical intimacy in marriage. Women are angered in the same way when there is a lack of good communication.

When both husbands and wives practice the art of good and positive communication, the knife effect will be eliminated. If one spouse isn't willing to work together with the other, the healing process can begin with one. Coming into this understanding will make a difference in every marriage.

1Peter 3:7 says: *"Likewise, ye husbands dwell with them according to knowledge giving honor unto the wife, as unto the weaker vessel and as being heirs together of the grace of life, that your prayers be not hindered."*

Dealing with a wife according to knowledge will begin the healing process. God gave Vedia this revelation to help bring understanding and healing to all marriages and families in the Body of Christ. Today I am pleased to say that I am a happy husband and I wouldn't trade my wife for any other! She is more beautiful to me today than the first day I met her.

LaVergne, TN USA
15 March 2010
175937LV00002B/2/P